The Afterlife

The Afterlife

Barry MacKinnon

THE AFTERLIFE

Copyright © 2020 Barry MacKinnon.

All rights reserved. No part of this book may be used or reproduced by any means, graphic, electronic, or mechanical, including photocopying, recording, taping or by any information storage retrieval system without the written permission of the author except in the case of brief quotations embodied in critical articles and reviews.

The views expressed in this work are solely those of the author and do not necessarily reflect the views of the publisher, and the publisher hereby disclaims any responsibility for them.

iUniverse books may be ordered through booksellers or by contacting:

iUniverse
1663 Liberty Drive
Bloomington, IN 47403
www.iuniverse.com
1-800-Authors (1-800-288-4677)

Because of the dynamic nature of the internet, any web addresses or links contained in this book may have changed since publication and may no longer be valid. The views expressed in this work are solely those of the author and do not necessarily reflect the views of the publisher, and the publisher hereby disclaims any responsibility for them.

Any people depicted in stock imagery provided by Getty Images are models, and such images are being used for illustrative purposes only.
Certain stock imagery © Getty Images.

ISBN: 978-1-5320-9103-2 (sc)
ISBN: 978-1-5320-9104-9 (e)

Print information available on the last page.

iUniverse rev. date: 02/21/2020

INTRODUCTION

This book has been a journey for me, and I have taken the time to question what life is and how mankind can improve it. I want to make a difference and leave a footprint for others to follow.

It was my aim to keep this book extremely brief and to the point. Many books that I have read were long and boring, with many pages of useless material. Hopefully my book is one that you can read many times.

I have a university degree and three college diplomas. I am the top person in the world in the establishment of a Center for the Life Extension Sciences. The life extension sciences are gerontology, transportation, artificial organology, regeneration, resuscitation, developmental biology, suspended animation, identity reconstruction, and a new science that I am introducing called cognitive reproduction and restoration. There are seven sciences in the United States and eight in

Canada (developmental biology being the eighth). The new science I will be introducing, cognitive reproduction and restoration, brings the total to nine.

The Center for the Life Extension Sciences will be the first of its kind in the world. People will come from around the globe to see and experience it. The center is a complete package and a one-stop learning experience for anyone seeking information on the sciences. The center is first and foremost a research facility with the potential to expand nationally and globally with new breakthroughs and advancements in the sciences. The center will create thousands of new jobs across Canada and tens of thousands of new jobs throughout the world.

I committed the better part of my life to trying to discover new ways to save and extend life. I am a common person with flaws like anybody else, maybe more. The support of my spouse was imperative when I ventured into this undertaking. I am fortunate to have an understanding wife who is as beautiful on the inside as she is on the outside. She is Christian and tolerant of my views. Thanks to her, I will continue to honor life and work diligently to save it.

Life extension is becoming more evident in our everyday lives with such widely known advancements as Baby Faye, William Schroeder, and Lindsay Eberhart, to name a few. Everyone tends to know someone whose life was extended by modern medical science. Many of these same people would have died on the operating table fifty years ago, but today, with all the progress in prolonging lives, the opportunity has been granted to them to continue to enjoy life. This is nothing compared to the progress that is possible with the sciences working as one. The Center for the Life Extension Sciences will show the world the importance of the new variables of life that the sciences can deliver.

You will see several things mentioned more than once in this book. This is intentional, as I hope to see you walk away with not only key information but life itself. Some people may disagree with me repeating things, but it is my book.

The philosophy behind my thinking is simple: if you can preserve the human body, you can rebuild it. At some point, we may not have to rebuild as often, thanks to gerontology.

There will obviously be a clash between my thinking and religion, but I will not be the destroyer of religion. If there is a destroyer, it will be truth. It is time for certain religions to go into a cocoon and come out presenting themselves differently. I don't wish to see religions destroyed but rather to see them altered. Even without a god, there is much good in religions.

There are many cycles to life, not just one, and the center will prove it and change forever the way mankind views life and death. It is a medical fact that when a person dies, they are still 99 percent alive in that all their organs and tissues are still intact. But what is being done about it? Mankind is cremating people or putting them in boxes and burying them. This makes perfectly good sense if you are mentally insane. Of all things on this planet, death is the most misunderstood and misused. This book aims to change your thinking when it comes to death. Death is a form of life. The trouble is mankind sees it as an end rather than a beginning.

A clergyman once held out both palms and said, "The value of life on earth is equal to the value of life in heaven." I was impressed with his comparison because it took some thought. I will try to give you a poor example of the value of one second of life, anybody's life. From the time you are born to the time you die, you pay a million dollars for every second of your life.

When you die at a ripe old age, all those millions are added up. Think how many times this immense figure would be to Mars and back. Now take this immense figure and make it equal to a drop of water and place it in the oceans of this world. Finish adding it up. Now you know why I am fighting so hard to promote this greatest of gifts. Well? Do you change life or wait till it changes you? Together, we can do our part to change the world in a significant way.

I believe in the potential of young minds when they're given the freedom to think new. I have the vision, and they have the imagination to nurture it. The center's new variables of life will improve mankind's quality of life for many centuries to come. Deep space exploration will be made possible by the center's new variables of life. I predict that the center will become one of the major tourist destinations in North America and the world. Who in their right minds wouldn't be interested in extended life, new options that avert death, a better quality of life, and the prospect of immortality?

When reading this book, it's very important to think about what happened to Christ's body after the cross. Christianity hinges on it.

There are two major parts to this book. The first is an autobiography providing the reader with a clear understanding of my early years and what it was like growing up in old Charlottetown on Prince Edward Island. The second part focuses on establishing a center for the life extension sciences that would be the first of its kind in the world. The second portion of my book aims to attract the attention of the wealthy who would sponsor the construction of the center.

Chapter 1

EARLY YEARS

CHILDHOOD

I was born on September 21, 1947, at the old Prince Edward Hospital in Charlottetown on Prince Edward Island.

One fine summer's day, my mother fed me and put me in my cradle to sleep. Then my father and mother took my older brother and walked up the street. The kitchen window was open, and a breeze blew the curtains onto a hot stove. Instantly, a fire erupted. A passerby saw the flames and smoke and phoned the fire department. The fire department was about a city block away, and the firemen were on the scene quickly. One fireman found me and took me outside while the others worked quickly to put out the flames. Their quick actions saved our home, my

Barry MacKinnon

mother's business, and me. Well, you've heard the expression of the cat with nine lives. This was number *one*.

I grew up in old Charlottetown when many of the old landmarks and historic sites were still standing or void of modern change. The city had personality in those days and was a grand old place to live and grow up. A park close by had a big gazebo and lots of flowers. There was none of the modern flare thrown in to dilute it.

My family lived in a Catholic neighborhood where my mother operated a dress shop on Grafton Street. Those were the days. Her first cash register was a shoe box. A salesman came in one day, looked around, and said she wouldn't be in business a week. She was still in business thirty-five years later. I wonder if the salesman could say the same.

From the front doorstep of the dress shop, I could look across the street and watch the nuns hurrying down the sidewalk to the Rochford Street Convent. The nuns always seemed to have a mystery to them. The Catholic Church was strong in those days, and its influence was felt in the community. How other kids and I loved climbing the nuns' cherry trees and helping ourselves to a feed. The nuns would come out with their brooms and chase us, but they always seemed to forgive us. Later in the afternoon, we would go down behind the convent and bum cookies from them. Those nuns could really cook, but at times they had mean tempers.

Even when I was just old enough to walk, I would take off on my own when my mother wasn't looking. One day, I walked for blocks until two black women found me wandering around the city and somehow brought me home. All I can remember is that they had big breasts. Have you ever tried to see a face from that angle with big breasts in the way?

There are more black people in our city today, but there

The Afterlife

were a lot less in those days. One black lady who lived a stone's throw away used to come over and babysit my brother and me. I used to watch as she whipped up potatoes like whipped cream. Man, were they good. My mother used to give her dresses in exchange for looking after us. She was a cleaner at the governor general's mansion at Victoria Park up until she retired. My mother told me that when she died, she had a big funeral, one as big as her heart. Sometimes you can't tell whether a person is black or white; all you can see is the person. At times, I wish we could see the world through the eyes of children.

I encountered death at an early age when I followed a little friend into a wake. In those days, wakes were frequently held in the home of the deceased. I remember kneeling beside the coffin, looking at a young boy who had been decapitated in an accident. It was a strange feeling. I had many encounters with death over the years, including Sister Mary Henry, whose coffin I watched being taken from the Rochford Street Convent. Death was strange to me. The only thing I knew about it was the horrible feeling of loss that crept over me.

At an early age, I ran the streets of Charlottetown, from city hall with its eighty-foot tower and mansard roof completed in 1888, to the railway station built in 1907, to Notre Dame Convent school for girls completed in 1857, to Government House, the official residence of the lieutenant governor, built in 1834.

I used to jump roofs at the Charlottetown wharf until one day I missed and ended up falling ten to twelve feet and landing on my back. I could have landed on my head or neck. It's a hell of a feeling having the wind knocked out of you and staring skyward, hoping for a breath of air. For a moment there, I thought I was a goner, but then I began to breathe again. This was number *two*.

Barry MacKinnon

In a pond behind the old West Kent School, I used to jump on blocks of ice during the wintertime. I didn't know how to swim at that time or the depth of the water. A sudden miss and it could be game over. This was number *three*. The government tore down that fine old brick building and erected the modern government buildings in its place. When will politicians learn to make new buildings but keep the old and give them a second use?

I wasn't Catholic, but I could bless myself with the best of them. Some of the Doyle boys who lived next to the convent were teaching me the Rosary when their mother came out, grabbed the rosary, and went back inside. She was a grand old soul who raised a lot of children. It's still a mystery how she did it. The convent seemed to be a hub of activity during the day, but the night belonged to the Rolloway down the street. It had a bowling alley on the bottom level and a dance hall on the second. I will always remember the big dance floor and the light in the ceiling that produced many different colors.

I frequently attended my mother's dress shop because she had to look after me and run the store. I was standing in the doorway when a little friend came up to me and told me about a sprinkler system that was going a few buildings down the street. Unbeknownst to my mother, off went my clothes and down the street I went. I must have been one of the first streakers in Charlottetown and put a few smiles on the faces of the nuns. Nothing was going to stop me, for it was a hot day.

Usually, when my mother would look out the dress shop windows, I would be on my knees, coughing my guts out. I had coughing and foot problems in my early years. I knew what a mustard plaster felt like. The heat on my chest was intense, to say the least.

The old legion across the street from my mother's dress shop

The Afterlife

was an interesting place to walk through, but I remember its roof more than anything because I used to climb from it to the next building using its chimney. I could see my mother's dress shop across the street, but it was a good thing she didn't see me. I was three stories up, but it never crossed my mind that this could be dangerous. This was number *four*.

From the legion's roof, I could gaze around the city and look at the drunks in the back, talking with no one listening. I could easily see the Charlottetown Hotel, which was built in the Georgian Revival style. It was first named the Canadian National at its completion in 1931. Its name was changed to the Charlottetown Hotel in 1939. From the legion's rooftop, I could also watch the milkman coming up the street with his horse and wagon. Man, how I loved chocolate milk in those small glass bottles. As I looked around, I could see my favorite building as well, the Prince Edward Cinema, which was built around 1895 and was an opera house at one time.

I didn't have a lot of money as a kid, but when I did, it was off to the movies. When I didn't have any money, it was still off to the movies. Once inside this grand old building, the floor slanted upward to two large doors at each end. The ticket booth was in the middle along the right side. Getting past the ticket booth was easy, but the big man collecting tickets at one of the two doors presented another problem. Two of us would rush in through the other door, which would bring the large man over to stop us. Then it was the other boys' turn to run through the opposite door. I didn't figure out until later that he wasn't trying to stop us, because once we were inside, he didn't bother with us. He was just putting on a show of his own.

One night, my mother woke my brother and me up to watch as the old Prince Edward Cinema went up in flames. It was quite the fire, as the wind carried the flames across the street and over our building. That was a really sad day in my life, for I had such an attachment to the old place. There was still the Capital Theater approximately two city blocks away, but it was nowhere close in grandeur to the Prince Edward. The Capital Theater is still standing and is presently being used by the Confederation Center of the Arts.

I learned to swim when I was knocked into the Charlottetown harbor. It was either sink or swim, so I kicked my legs and moved my arms until I got to a ladder and climbed up. Some kids may not have been so lucky. If I had been in an area with no ladder, exhaustion would have overtaken me. This was number *five*.

The first school I attended was the old West Kent. There was no gym, and everyone used to go up to the top floor to meet. I remember being put over a teacher's legs and smacked. I loved being smacked because I got a better look at her legs. One day, another boy threw a book at me, so I returned the favor. Just as my book was in the air, the principal walked in. The book just missed his nose. My life flashed before my eyes as I stood there, shaking, waiting for his response. To my surprise, he turned and slowly walked out of the room. Needless to say, I never again threw a book. I even lived long enough to carry the bell around the school to let everyone know it was time to go to class.

I lived less than a city block from Queen's Square, which in my opinion represented the most unique part of the city. There were five buildings in a row along Grafton Street that were all different in design and purpose. Some of these buildings shared similar duties over the years. The first building was the Market House, built around 1904, which succumbed to fire in 1958. It was here that farmers brought their goods for sale. The next building was the post office, built in 1887 and named the

The Afterlife

Cabot Building. Next to the Cabot Building and in the center of the square stood the stone Colonial Building, now called Province House, which was completed in 1847. It was used for judicial and legislative purposes; it was here that the fathers of confederation met to create the nation of Canada.

Next to Province House was the Law Courts Building, often called the courthouse, which was built in 1876. A fire in 1976 caused extensive damage to the building, but it was rebuilt and used to house the Public Archives of Prince Edward Island. The building is now called the Honorable George Coles Building. Next to the old Law Courts Building is St. Paul's Anglican Church. This church was built of island sandstone and is now surrounded by large old trees.

In front of these five buildings were lots of fine old trees, which made it a wonderful place to go for a stroll. In 1958, the Market House burned down and the Cabot Building was demolished to make way for the Confederation Center of the Arts and library complex, which was built in 1964. How any politician could be stupid enough to erect such a modern complex in the heart of old Charlottetown is beyond all comprehension.

A must-see in old Charlottetown is the All Souls Chapel, which is attached to St. Peter's Cathedral on Rochford Street. It's about two blocks from my mother's dress shop. In case I forgot to mention it, her brick building is still on Grafton Street. The chapel was begun in 1888, and the artist Robert Harris enhanced it with some of his paintings. It is a very small chapel, but it offers a heartwarming experience. I found it nice just to sit there for a while and feel the past around me.

St. Dunstan's Basilica, finished in 1919, was built in the form of a Gothic cross. With its two-hundred-foot spires, it is easily visible on the city skyline. It is still the largest Catholic

Barry MacKinnon

church on the island. I often wandered through it with my friends who were Catholic. I always found it quite strange to watch people entering the tiny booths to talk with a priest; for some friends I had to wait awhile.

A city block from St. Dunstan's Basilica is Trinity United Church, completed in 1864. Trinity is the oldest church building still being used in Charlottetown, and it was the church our family attended. The section of the building that I loved playing in burned down, but the main structure is still standing with a new addition. There are many churches in the city that are a must to experience. My wife and I used to visit a different church every Sunday during the summer months when we first married. In certain churches we felt a little strange, but the people were always friendly.

I was a happy kid who loved to play sports. Several children in my neighborhood loved to play baseball, so I joined the city baseball league at Victoria Park. When I was fourteen, I tried out for the minor league all-star team and was playing first base with a big outfielder's glove when the shortstop threw a fast one. I had to reach for the ball, and it hit the inside of my glove and popped back out. I remember being in considerable pain, and when I took my glove off, one of my fingers was almost Z-shaped. I walked over to Forby, who played in the National Hockey League. I said, "I guess I can't play," and showed him my finger. He gave it a quick look and then gave it a yank. He told me to get back on first and then yelled, "Play ball!" I still remember what Forby told my brother about a fella who always tried to run over him on third base: "The way to curb this problem is to take the ball like this and plant it in the guy's face. Next time, he'll slide." It was a tough league.

Hockey was a favorite winter sport of mine, and I can remember one game in particular at the old Charlottetown

The Afterlife

Forum. The other team had this guy whose back porch light was burnt out. He was all over the ice with his stick everywhere except on the ice. I was going after a loose puck when suddenly the blade of a stick struck me just beneath my bottom lip. It went right through to my teeth. It could have been my eyes or throat because we didn't wear head or face guards in those days. I continued playing with my bleeding face until one of the coaches told me to go to the office. I was taken to the hospital for stitches. This was number *six*. The other guy was never allowed on the ice again.

There was a brief period when I hung around with a poor group of kids that were not from my neighborhood. We used to go into stores and steal just for the hell of it. One corner store that was owned by a Jewish or Lebanese family always stuck in my mind. I wanted to go back and drop a twenty down behind the counter when the owner wasn't looking. However, he died and the store changed hands, so I never got an opportunity to say I was sorry.

My youth was a wonderful time. Every weekend our family would go to our cottage on Tracadie Bay. My mother would work in her dress shop all week and look forward to the peace and quiet that the bay offered. Nights were special, as the frogs in the nearby pond sounded their joy of the evening. It was an isolated spot, and the night air enhanced a good night's sleep. We had no toilets or running water, but this didn't seem to bother us. There was a cool spring about a city block away that had great tasting water. Each day, we had to take our bucket and get our daily supply. It was a wonderful place, for the bay provided an abundance of mussels, clams, and oysters. The food always seemed to taste so good, especially after a good swim.

It was on Tracadie Bay that my sport of killing came to an end. My father bought me a one-shot .22 caliber rifle that I

Barry MacKinnon

took to the cottage. He experienced the war and felt I should know. One day, a friend and I had only two bullets left when we saw what looked like a crane out in the bay. This bird was a good city block away when my friend fired, and we could see the bullet hit the water fifteen feet from it. Seeing my friend miss and realizing I had only one bullet left, I really took my time before squeezing the trigger. The rifle went off, but we didn't see the bullet strike the water. Even from that distance we could tell there was something wrong with the bird. We walked up the shore toward it, and as we approached, several other birds flew off. The bird that I shot was dragging a wing and looked at us as if asking why and what it had ever done to us. A shot from my rifle had changed this bird's life.

We realized the bird couldn't survive in this condition and that leaving it was not an option. We killed that poor bird with rocks, covered it, and walked away. My thoughts flashed back to an earlier time when I killed a pigeon with a wire slingshot. The pigeon was only six feet away when I quickly turned and fired. The staple hit the pigeon in the back of its head. I was close enough to see its eyes roll back. The pigeon died instantly. The bird at our cottage was the last bird I killed. Killing for sport is so wrong, and I carry my stupidity to this day. An animal's life is as valuable to it as mine is to me.

Each day at the cottage, I always made a trip up to the old MacKinnon homestead, situated about two city blocks from our cottage. The farm used to be owned by Sir William MacDonald, the tobacco king. He named the farm after the Glenaladale MacDonalds, who migrated to the island in 1772. Prince Edward Island back then was called the Isle de St. Jean, and Tracadie Bay was called the Bedford Bay. The MacDonald house has been standing for more than a century. It was made of bricks and stood fifty feet square and three stories high with a mansard slated roof, which has now been changed to shingles. It was finished from cellar to garret in the finest style of carpentry and was acknowledged to be one of the finest county residences in the province. The first floor is divided into five rooms with a spacious hall running the entire length of the building. The second floor is divided into seven bedrooms, with an L-shaped hall. The third floor is broken into rooms to accommodate servants.

The different rooms of the residence are splendidly proportioned and elegantly furnished. In front of the dwelling is a veranda that is ten feet wide. The windows are protected by Venetian shutters. The house is still standing today and is open to the public. I slept in the small room next to the master bedroom.

The original barn was 277 feet long, fifty-two feet broad—except in the center, where it was seventy-six feet broad—and fifty-six feet high. At the time it was built, it was the largest barn in Canada. The barn was connected to the house by a three-hundred-foot enclosure. In 1907, the barn burned down and was replaced with a barn that was 150 feet by fifty-two feet. This barn fell down in the early 1990s, but I will always remember the fun times I had jumping into piles of hay or just watching the various farm animals. One day, I was on the back of the tractor when my father was rolling a field. He happened to look behind him just as the roller was up to my neck. This was number *seven*.

Sir William MacDonald was born at Glenaladale on Prince Edward Island. He left the island in 1854 and moved to Montreal, Quebec, where he became a commission merchant. Sir William made millions as a tobacco merchant and manufacturer. During his lifetime, he endowed colleges and universities across Canada. He gave McGill University approximately $11 million dollars. This alone made him the greatest benefactor to education in Canada's history. His total donations to education are estimated at more than $17 million.

In 1905, the property was put up for sale and was purchased by the MacKinnon family, who owned it until recently. Much of the MacKinnon wealth was acquired during the rum running days. A ship used to come into Tracadie Bay and unload. On one occasion, there was more than twenty thousand dollars' worth of liquor on the front lawn. A lot of money in those days. There were eleven children in the MacKinnon family, and I remember my mother telling me that Mrs. MacKinnon was the nicest old soul you could ever meet. Even in her eighties, she was still pulling buckets of milk back from the barn.

Adolescence

My brother was a good student and went on to study for the Governor General's Award, for which he came second. I seemed to be more interested in sports than school, even though I knew I would never become a professional athlete. Once in grade eight, I thought about quitting school because other kids were doing it. It wasn't until grade nine that I decided to make something of my life. My education was uphill the hard way. People can change and grow if the desire is there.

I remember Trinity United Church well, for I sang in the boys' choir and attended Cub Scouts and so forth. I remember the church vividly, with the sun flowing through its high colored windows as the minister's voice carried throughout the building. Many times I sat in the boys' choir, watching and listening as the minister's voice commanded attention. The church had a large balcony that almost went completely around it and beautiful stained glass windows. In those days,

The Afterlife

the church was crowded with a good mixture of young and old. One Sunday, my family and I went to church and sat up in the balcony. When I looked down, I recognized an older gentleman who used to teach Sunday school many years earlier. It's strange how certain people stand out in your memory. I remember teaching Sunday school at Trinity for a number of years and, on occasion, speaking briefly from the pulpit. Even at a young age, I contemplated joining the ministry.

Adolescence is a time of the changing of the guard. New friends are acquired. One friend I met at this time was Vernon. He lived with his mother and brother in a small house with a clay floor. Vernon was his own person. Although poor, he learned to play the mouth organ and a guitar that he made from parts. He could also draw well enough to win an art competition. He couldn't go because of money. He had one black pair of pants that he ironed frequently. He had a crease in them that could cut butter. He was a good person who didn't swear or look for fights. What this fellow could have become if his situation had been different.

I hung around with different youth now. Two in particular were good students. We did a lot together, including going to summer camp. We broke out one night and had the camp supervisors chase us up the coast. Everything was an adventure. I was older than they were because of the grades I had failed. I never did good in school because of French. In those days, if you failed one subject, you failed them all. I knew that I was going to fail before the year began. I didn't like French, and each year I fell further behind. I failed four or five years because of it. One day, the principal called me into his office and told me that I was not university material. He said I should get out of school and take up a trade. It was decent advice, since I was always at the bottom of my class thanks to French.

One evening when I got home, I told my mother that the principal had advised me to quit school. She got upset because she never had an opportunity to acquire a good education. Knowing my mother, she must have had some choice words with the principal. She told me that I was going on, and that was that. I began sitting behind the brains in the class and began working harder at my studies once I heard you could go to university as a mature student. Needless to say, French would no longer be on my agenda. Years later, I met up with the principal and told him my education level. He never said a word. I wonder if he realized that he lived his life in a box, a victim of the system. The thought of sticking his neck out and changing the system never crossed his mind.

I remembered one teacher in particular who taught math and was a farmer, a big fellow with muscles. I was in his class when he called a student up to check his work. The student obviously didn't have his homework done correctly and received a shake for it. Next, the teacher called up the student in front of me. He gave him a violent shake and tossed him over by the wall. He looked at me, and I looked at him. I waited for him to call my name, for I was going to run out of the class. I had no intention of going through the wall. Luckily for me, he never called my name. He wouldn't have caught me anyway.

Most kids in my class never bothered me because I was older. However, one guy who was over six feet tall tried. I grabbed him and pinned him up against a wall. He never bothered me after that.

I loved playing school sports, but the principal eventually kicked me out of them because of my age. Sitting in the bleachers and watching others play didn't bother me. I turned my attention to my studies. I took all the help I could get from other students. The thought of entering university as a mature student gave me new hope, so I began focusing on my studies. I tried cigarette smoking and drugs only once. They just didn't interest me.

I was fifteen years old when my parents finally divorced. It was a sad time for me. I learned that my mother had been raped by her father and that her mother had died at an early age. No wonder my mother drank so heavily for most of her life. How does a young girl put that behind her? She moved to Montreal when she was fifteen and worked tables.

Another person I hung around with at this time was Mike. When Mike's father was dying, it took four nurses to hold him in the bed. He didn't want to go. Too bad others didn't enjoy life as much as his father. Mike and I shared a lot and did many things together. One day, we were driving back to Charlottetown from the farm in Tracadie when my front left tire exploded. Instantly, I grabbed the steering wheel with both hands and pulled it hard to the left. The car went as straight as an arrow until it stopped. The car had been shaken to pieces. The tire, wheel, radiator, etc., was shattered and required new parts. I could have easily hit another car or truck or rolled my car, but I didn't. Both Mike and I walked away without a scratch. This was number *eight*.

In my late adolescence, I began to get interested in church and church groups at Trinity United in Charlottetown. I met with the minister about going into the ministry, and he began molding me for a career in it. He had me doing more church work and attending older men's conferences. I began attending church on a regular basis.

I taught Sunday school and got involved in church groups. Whenever I could fit in and acquire new skills, I took advantage of the opportunity. I decided on my eighteenth birthday to finally go into the ministry. It was only several months away.

At one particular older men's conference, I was the youngest there. I listened as retired men got up to speak about the deaths of their spouses. One man reminded me of a sergeant in the army. Suddenly, he began crying like a baby and had to sit down. He must have loved his wife dearly, and he obviously missed her presence in his life. He was not the only one to break into tears over the loss of his wife.

I sat there listening to the various speakers, and when the sessions were through for the night, I went on a solitary walk along the shore. It was pitch-black and windy, and I could hear the waves breaking upon the shore. The wind was so fierce that it blew my hair everywhere. From nowhere came a question: Is there really a God? The question surprised me. I had never asked it before. Suddenly, I had to know the answer before committing my life to the service of God. I thought it a formality and just a matter of going around a corner and there would be my answer. Problem solved! I met with my minister, who was surprised. We talked for a while, and then I left. I was not satisfied with his answers, so I went searching for God.

Chapter 2

MY LIFE'S STAGES

CHRISTIAN

I continued to search for God. My thoughts of going into the ministry were put on a back burner. I couldn't go into the ministry with any doubts on my mind. I started reading the Bible from cover to cover, hoping to find the solution to my problem. In the back portion of the Bible, I read the sentence, "Most Christians are in dense ignorance regarding the most fundamental doctrines of their own faith." After that, I became choosier about who I asked for advice. There is obviously more to being a Christian than just going to church or saying you are one.

I began reading anything I could get my hands on, hoping that the elusive information I sought existed somewhere. I still went to church regularly. I enjoyed a good sermon. I listened to

Billy Graham and others on television. One guy on television ended up going to prison. He put on a good show only to get wealthy. I quickly discovered that you couldn't believe everything a person said. The majority of people have good and fair minds. I did a lot of thinking at this time.

Agnostic

The longer I went without going into the ministry, the more self-doubt crept into my mind. One day I was a Christian and the next an agnostic. I began reading Christian and non-Christian material. My contentment as a person was being tested. It seemed that I was going nowhere fast. I was no longer confined to one belief and could see things in a new light. With this new thinking came new consequences. Gradually, I lost contentment. I used to wake like a flower unfolding its petals to the early morning sun, but things were changing. My love of life was diminishing.

Land of the Living Dead

Then came the land of the living dead, as I call it. For a short time, I didn't care about anyone or anything, especially myself. Saying I was confused is putting it mildly. I felt alone and isolated with a sick mind. Should I go to a psychiatrist and receive treatment, or should I continue alone? The psychiatrist would have been a quick fix but may have left me dependent on him or her.

My mind raced in all directions and would often shut down. I spent a lot of time in a twisting chair. I would go for a walk only to end up back in the twisting chair. I kept my family members that were close to me in the dark as I continued along, void of support. At this time, if a person hung around with the wrong crowd, it could be fatal. Luckily for me, I didn't. I was also fortunate that this period lasted only a short time. I am certain that many people are not so lucky.

ATHEIST

Accepting myself as an atheist was a gradual process. One just doesn't jump into it. There was the possibility of going back to becoming a Christian, or so I believed. What were the advantages of becoming an atheist? Besides saying you don't believe in God, what is there? Did I expect people to clap me on the back and say how brave I was? When we die, is that it? I was on the outs as far as other people were concerned. I remember getting into an argument with my mother concerning the existence of God. At the time, she won the argument by saying, "Even if you could prove there is no God, I still wouldn't believe you." So I shut my mouth and avoided getting into religious conversations with people. However, I didn't know then what I know now.

I used to blame God for everything, but it was like blaming a broom for too much dirt to clean up. The problem was me, and I had to learn to first blame myself.

When I married, my wife was Christian and still is. I thought it would definitely complicate things, but it didn't. I don't share my religious views verbally with her. I wrote a number of articles on various subjects, and she was always helpful in perusing them. I appreciated her taking the time to edit them. I started going to church again with her. To my surprise, I still enjoyed a good sermon and got some good out of attending church. I enjoyed the fellowship and meeting people.

IMMORTALIST

The immortalist stage is the last I entered. There are only a few of us in the world, but someday there will be many. We are a special breed who feel that there are many cycles to life, not just one, and that immortality is a possibility if we're willing to work for it. Personally, I don't believe in God, but I dislike atheists. They are afraid or don't know about immortalism. I believe in taking from all religions and beliefs, anything that will make me into a better human being. All religions and beliefs have valuable material; one just has to find it. Maybe I am too bold in my thinking and the general person needs to see a reality (the Center for the Life Extension Sciences) or another option before they can be swayed.

I felt that the immortalist belief suited me as a person, and I felt complete again. I could enter any church and enjoy myself as long as I could understand what they were saying. One has to learn to choose what you want to believe. It's this picking and choosing of material that separates you from other people. As the world evolves, more religions will adapt themselves to immortalism's presence. The immortalist can adjust more quickly to mixed marriages, and this will become easier as the world changes and the number of immortalists in religious congregations grows.

Chapter 3

THE TWO ASSOCIATIONS

THE CANADIAN LIFE EXTENSION ASSOCIATION

*M*y attitude concerning life was changing, and I no longer wanted to be an observer. I wanted to be a participant. Life is too important to sit in the shadows of others. I wanted to do something, but what?

The first thing to cross my mind was to create a nonprofit, so I founded the Canadian Life Extension Association. On January 1, 1983, it became a registered charity with Revenue Canada. Its logo consisted of a maple leaf with a pyramid in it. The pyramid is a symbol of humankind's first attempt to stop death. The association's main objective was to establish an information center for the life extension sciences. This one-stop shop for information on the life extension sciences would be the first of its kind in the world. It would house a wealth of knowledge, including information on

- the latest breakthroughs and advances in a particular science,
- equipment involved in the research,
- people and institutions deserving recognition,
- techniques now being used,
- countries and institutions undertaking research,
- future hopes, and
- special books and resources on the sciences.

People would need to go no further than the Center for the Life Extension Sciences, for it would be a good quality service containing a storehouse of information. Back in the 1980s, the complex would have cost $12 million to build. The corporations and foundations we contacted for funding at the time were donating to cancer research and had no available funds for a young organization advocating something new. Because of people like Terry Fox, many of the organizations I contacted were giving to cancer research. I guess people felt a cure was just around the corner. I couldn't even get scraps from cancer's table.

No organization to date has attempted or succeeded in becoming a major information center and showroom for all eight sciences: gerontology, transplantation, artificial organology, identity reconstruction, regeneration, resuscitation, suspended animation, and developmental biology. There are seven life extension sciences in the United States and eight in Canada (developmental biology is the eighth). Stark, Hicks, and Spraggle—an architect firm in Mississauga, Ontario—did the initial blueprints for the center on speculation. I wrote a report that was more than a hundred pages in length and

The Afterlife

decided to mail it out to determine interest. Again, people were not interested in funding such a facility.

The center would encourage people to want more responsibility for their own lives and futures; enable the Canadian Life Extension Association to raise capital that would be spent on promoting medical research in all the sciences; and make large numbers of people aware of the potential within the sciences.

After several years, my efforts proved futile, and I had to terminate the association. I was ready to throw in the towel. I remember writing to a person, saying, "I had placed my small stone along the path leading to immortality and disappeared into the mist of time, knowing that I made it a little easier for those coming behind. Now it is up to people like you to drop the remaining stones."

For a short time, I gave up, but no one took my place. But failure only prompted me to fight harder, and I continued on alone, expanding the center concept and seeking out those who might support it. Any person can spit out negative remarks about an endeavor, but it's the person who stays the course who will make a difference. There are two kinds of people one can support: the kind who want to climb a mountain and the kind who believe they can. I believe I can or I would have given up years ago.

If I had to do it over, I would amass great wealth. The trouble with amassing great wealth is that it takes time and commitment. One has to live, eat, and shit with it on his or her mind until the only contentment comes from success or death. Anything else is a waste of time. To build a concept like the center demands the same commitment. Trying to accomplish both at the same time is futile. It's like trying to live with a mistress and a wife. I am now too old to start amassing great wealth and must rely on others if the center concept is to succeed.

I always hoped that we would live during a time when money was not more intelligent than intelligence itself.

The Center for the Life Extension Sciences

After an extensive exploration of the center idea, I decided to take it a step further. I would build a *research* center for the life extension sciences that would be the first of its kind in the world. In other words, I would unite the sciences. Only this time, I would include a new science called cognitive reproduction and restoration.

I believe there can be no peace in the world or the universe until the value of life has been truly learned, appreciated, and lived to the fullest. We must all realize that in order to support peace, we must first learn to promote life.

The Center for the Life Extension Sciences will commit itself to enhancing human life. The center will be a major source of information for all the sciences. Upon its completion, I urge you to visit and experience a tour of this unique facility. If the center does become a reality, please add it to your list of deserving organizations that you support. The challenge of the center is to awaken humankind to the vast potential in human life that lies ahead.

I have included a brief definition of each of the sciences to help in your understanding of them:

- *Gerontology*—the study of aging

- *Transplantation*—the transfer of an organ or tissue from one part of an individual to another (heart, kidney, liver, etc.)
- *Artificial organology*—the removal of damaged or nonfunctional organs and replacing them with artificial ones (artificial arms, legs, etc.)
- *Identity reconstruction*—a colony or group of organisms that have arisen from a single individual as a result of asexual reproduction (cloning of skin, etc.).
- *Regeneration*—the restoration of segments of an animal body after damage or loss (blood vessel proliferation)
- *Resuscitation*—the revival of a person from a condition resembling death
- *Suspended animation*—the cessation of the vital functions temporarily (cryobiology, cryonics, etc.).
- *Developmental biology*—the study of the life cycles of organisms from fertilization to death
- *Cognitive reproduction and restoration*—the reproduction and restoration of the mental processes of perception, memory, judgment, and reasoning

As you can see, there are now nine life extension sciences. I know that at some point in time, some sciences will make others obsolete and new ones may be added, but for now, all sciences are important, though some more than others.

The life extension sciences and their new variables of life are the doorway to new life options. People must be made aware of life's new options, and the center will be the instrument that brings that information to the world.

The center is primarily a research facility and information center, but during the summer months it will open its gates to the world and reveal the new life options awaiting humankind.

If the center achieves only a fraction of what I think it can, many corporations and billionaires will regret their lack of involvement. When it comes to life, the ignorance of humankind has always scared me. It's not a matter of me being before my time as much as it is others missing theirs. I am an immortalist who knows where I am going; I only need a vehicle to get there. If only you could realize it, you are a catalyst that could help make things happen. Help me to help you.

The uniqueness of the center lies in its ability to move researchers and engineers quickly from one science to another in small or large numbers in order to instigate quicker results and to maintain a fresh minded approach. The sharing of information between the sciences will prove beneficial. Researchers and engineers may fail miserably in one science but shine in another. The center will stress extensive classroom work before lab work. The correct research direction is key to quick success.

Most of us sit back and let others become the instigator of our thoughts. Taking the first step for the good of humankind is not easy. The fear of being wrong is at the forefront of one's mind. What will others think? You must have the courage to be wrong, because you could be right. It is humankind's inability or refusal to think outside the box that prohibits him from enjoying an abundance of life. Where are you at? Certain trees can live for thousands of years, yet most humans can't make it to a hundred. There's something wrong with this picture.

Where does one build such a facility? If I were going to build something that would stand out, I would build it in a location where people wouldn't expect to find it and somewhere that would provide researchers with the quiet they deserve for a certain part of the year. Something like the

The Afterlife

Shrine of Sainte-Anne-de-Beaupre in Quebec, which I visited. I stood in awe of the structure, but when I entered, my mouth dropped open. When I exited the basilica, I stood staring at the surrounding houses, which were the size of cottages. How could they have built such a grand structure? They couldn't! The money had to come from somewhere else. From wealthy people or companies that had the vision to build it there. I envied the builders of the shrine and wished my center could receive similar support. I am worried over the response of one American billionaire; he said Americans will not support anything that's not built in their backyard. I hope he was not speaking for all Americans. The center is too important for such frivolous thinking.

I understand that Bill Gates gave at least $30 billion of his wealth to charities. It was a noble thing to do. The cost of the Center for the Life Extension Sciences is minuscule in comparison, but the center will have a greater impact and will touch the world like no other thing before it. Is ignorance so great that it keeps a person from becoming a part of this grand endeavor? Life is about to become the biggest industry on the planet, and the center will play a major role in instigating it.

People don't have to wait a thousand years or even five hundred years for the center's breakthroughs and advancements to occur. The goal of the center is to achieve many of them within a hundred years. The center will never allow its researchers or engineers the luxury that cancer researchers have received. Researchers will be fired quickly if they don't show imagination and positive results. Many of the researchers and engineers will come from the United States and Canada, but some will come from other countries, especially those that show substantial promise or special skills. The center will become a major employer within Prince Edward Island, Canada, and the world.

Chapter 4

THREE AREAS TO OVERCOME

In order for the Center for the Life Extension Sciences to be fully realized, three areas must be traversed, and in the following order: religion, medicine, finance.

RELIGION

Three areas within religion need to be addressed. The first is that people must remember that the Bible was written about one hundred years after the death of Christ. I was once part of a group of twelve people who sat in a row. The instructor whispered a sentence to the first person and asked him to pass it on to the next. By the time we reached the end of the line, the sentence was completely changed. Think how much a story would change in one hundred years.

Second is a so-called miracle. When Christ went out into the wilderness, the only food in the multitude that followed him was five loaves of bread and two fish. Christ broke up the food, and when everyone was through eating, there were enough crumbs left over to fill twelve baskets. Question! How many baskets does it take to carry five loaves and two fish? A maximum of seven. But there were enough crumbs left over to fill twelve baskets. Twelve minus seven leaves five. Where did those five baskets come from? A university professor who taught religion didn't have the answer. Each time he came up with a response, I would prove it wrong. After having him on the ropes and bleeding, I decided to go.

The third and most important thing is the death of Christ. Christ died on a cross with a criminal on either side of him. It was not like in the movies with Christ on a hill. He was on a road with hundreds of other criminals. The spear wound in his side was made by a Roman soldier checking to see if Christ was dead. The soldier was the only person who knew Christ's approximate time of death. The key thing that we must remember is that Christ's body was the property of Rome. After all, he was seen by Rome as a messiah. Rome's thinking on messiahs would change, but not for hundreds of years.

The first messiah was Simon, who was killed by Rome approximately forty years earlier. Simon and his followers defeated a Roman garrison. But Rome, being Rome, sent a larger army that defeated Simon and his followers. Simon was beheaded and left to rot where he fell. Roman soldiers guarded him so that Christians couldn't take the body. Christ was seen by Rome as a messiah, and his body wouldn't have been allowed to be taken by Christians. Rome saw the danger of a messiah. Much of Simon's thinking was passed on to Christ by his first cousin John the Baptist, who knew both messiahs.

The Afterlife

Early Christians, seeing the death of two messiahs, had to do something in a hurry. Christianity was at risk. The only thing open to them was to lie, and if you are going to lie, you may as well make it a good one. There was a large stone moved, angels, and a risen Christ. It was all a lie, but a lie is as good as the truth if you can find someone simple enough to believe it. It wasn't hard for people to believe because religion was the only game in town that offered immortality, but that is changing.

MEDICINE

For centuries, religion's dominance on immortality grew until modern times when men like Robert Ettinger, the father of cryonics, came on the scene, telling people that there were many cycles to life, not just one. In my darkest hour, Ettinger was the light at the end of my dark tunnel.

It is a medical fact that when a person dies, he or she is still 99 percent alive in that all of his or her body organs and tissues are still intact. But what does society do with people who are still 99 percent alive? It cremates them or puts them in boxes and buries them. It makes perfectly good sense if you are mentally insane. The world has been fooled for too long. Our attitude toward death will change because of the Center for the Life Extension Sciences. We will learn to use and control death. It will be our slave rather than our master.

I want to create a center for the life extension sciences that will change the world forever. I want to turn the negative attitude held toward traditional death and dying around. I want to take the myth of immortality and make it a reality. I want to unite the sciences, bringing the total to nine.

FINANCE

With many unique endeavors, the need for money arises. My major efforts have involved contacting corporations and the super rich. Originally, I thought of them as wealthy and having their own minds. I thought self-made people would value an idea that was unique and beneficial to humankind. They have the money to make things happen. I said anybody who told me that they wouldn't help with the construction of the Center for the Life Extension Sciences was full of shit and didn't know what they were talking about. I was wrong!

Billionaires can make money, but do they have enough intellect to save themselves? I contacted hundreds of them in the United States and globally, but not one offered to help. God belief was the only game in town for centuries, and at one time, I would have said to fill your boots with it, but no more. God belief will quickly fall into second place. It is said that Christ supposedly came back from the dead, but we now know better. The center will be responsible for bringing millions back to life. We will need these people for our settlements in space. Death is a form of life, and hopefully the center will be responsible for proving it. The world will soon set sail upon the universe, and humankind's many life cycles will go with it.

Maybe billionaires will have a change of heart when they see and read this book. Maybe they will rise to the occasion and be part of the greatest endeavor known to humankind. Common sense will tell them that what I have said will come about, if not by my hand, then by somebody else's. Burying their heads in the sand will not make it go away.

Chapter 5

Past and Future Plans for the Center

The following are some questions and comments that people may have about the Center.

Why is the center needed?

The Center for the Life Extension Sciences will open the eyes of many to new and wondrous things, and it will change the world forever. Here are ten key points on this topic:

1. The center will be the first of its kind in the world by uniting the sciences in one locale.

2. A new science called cognitive reproduction and restoration will be added, bringing the total number of sciences to nine.
3. If people don't cut it at work, they will be fired and fired quickly.
4. Unlike other institutions, the researchers and engineers may receive the opportunity to work in all nine sciences.
5. At a moment's notice, researchers and engineers could be temporarily moved in small or large numbers from one science to another if it would instigate quicker results.
6. The center will be first and foremost a research facility, but it will open its gates to the world for five months a year and serve as the center's major education tool.
7. Deep space exploration will be made possible because of the new variables of life that the center will offer.
8. Sharing information between the sciences will enhance and lead to better results.
9. At present, most people are choosing between two options: a coffin or a metal vase. The center will change that. It will prove to the world that there are many cycles to life, not just one.
10. Researchers and engineers at the center will receive free room and board, for much will be expected of them. Every aspect of research will have a timetable attached to it. Failure to succeed will mean getting fired, moved to another science, or transferred to another position at the center, if one is available.

WHAT GOALS WILL IT ACHIEVE?

The life extension sciences, acting as one, will provide new variables of life for humankind that will make deep space travel not only possible but probable. NASA could benefit substantially from the center's research.

The ultimate goal of the center is immortality. As soon as the center is constructed, humankind will be placed on the road to immortality. The four phases of the center will be (1) construction and staffing, (2) breakthroughs and advancements, (3) global expansion, and (4) immortality under certain conditions. The center will grow into something much larger than a research center. It will also house and train individuals to expand nationally and globally to meet the ever-changing needs of a world. New centers will be built on a much smaller scale to fill individuals' immediate needs. Choosing a suitable location for the Center is key to its success.

Will world leaders look differently upon their actions, knowing that they can return to a world full of life, not death? Will a new understanding of death save the world of tomorrow?

The center will have the power to change the direction of the world, and the one thing that should impress you is that the center's results will occur within a brief time period. Excuses will not be tolerated at the center.

Religious-minded individuals, in the beginning, will find my thinking difficult to accept. For centuries, they attended high and massive churches designed to impress and control. Truth, on the other hand, was pushed to the side or forced to hide its face and wait. The waiting is over, and the strongest churches must conform to the changes or suffer greatly for it.

There are many life cycles, not just one. A clash between religious immortality and that of the center is unavoidable, and the common person will be left to choose immortality in the bush offered by religions or immortality in the hand offered by the center. People will soon learn that the only thing standing between them and certain death is the center. My thinking may be hard for the common person to accept because for centuries religious immortality was the only game in town, but not anymore. Many people live their entire lives in an intellectual box owned and operated by religions, but now it is time to start burning these boxes, for there is a new alternative. One that is real, one that you can touch, and it will only get better with time.

We will soon set sail upon the universe, and coffins will be things of the past. Time capsules will be the new age with everything above ground. I previously mentioned above - and belowground patients. It may be easier to just clone underground patients and transfer thought. Humans are fortunate that we are not complicated, with much of our lives taken up by family, friends, work, church, hobbies, sports, cottages, and homes.

The aboveground patients should be easier to suspend, rebuild, and change because we have much more to work with, as the condition of a person's body has not been seriously altered by time. New advances and treatments will dictate the direction taken. Suspending an individual may not be a needed option. Advances in the sciences may make this process obsolete.

I fear we are living in a time when visionaries are being left on the doorstep of change and the so-called educated are walking in void of vision and imagination. At best, they are the keepers of other people's thinking. Hopefully this will change and people will soon take advantage of the many breakthroughs and advances that will occur within the sciences.

WHAT JOBS WILL IT CREATE?

Life is about to become the biggest industry on the planet, and the center will be the major instigator of it. The center will receive the recognition and gratitude of millions of people in the near future. People will walk around the center's grounds, marveling about what's to come next.

The financial spin-offs from the sciences will be great and create thousands of new job opportunities.

Once the science buildings are erected, staff will be required to fill them. Some of the staff that will be needed include

- general technicians,
- laborers,
- medical technicians,
- teachers,
- production clerks,
- machinery technicians, and
- shippers/receivers.

A lot depends on the needs within the various sciences. Related sciences that partner with one another may have similar job needs. Some examples of potential overlap would be

- identity reconstruction and cognitive reproduction and restoration;
- resuscitation and suspended animation;
- transplantation and regeneration; and
- developmental biology and identity reconstruction and regeneration.

Once operational, the center will have its own means for procuring funding. Income from the sciences will become the major revenue source. The lucrative spin-offs from the sciences will create revenue and thousands of new job opportunities. A province, state, or country should give generously when the center expands into it. Revenue will come from the ticket sales at the gate. Other sources of revenue will come from the food fair, merchandise store, and general fund raising, etc.

Many people will give generously to the center once they see it as a reality or a soon-to-be one. The center is capable of giving back much more than it receives, and it will do so in many different ways.

What will it cost?

Wealthy individuals, you have a decision to make! Either part with some of your great wealth and set the world of life into motion or do nothing and die. Only a handful of wealthy individuals are needed to change the world forever. As much as the wealthy have turned their backs to me, I still believe in them.

The wealthy will receive much from their participation with the Center for the Life Extension Sciences. They will acquire things that only the center can provide. Imagination determines what the future holds, and the generosity of billionaires and other wealthy individuals can make things happen much faster. What's in it for you? The answer is simple: life. There are other benefits, but life is the major one. For the intelligent person life will be enough.

Construction costs for the new center will be substantially reduced thanks to Stonemaker in Guelph, Ontario. The center will purchase its own brick- and block-making equipment, which will speed up construction and reduce costs.

I hope to satisfactorily prove that the foundation of religion (Christianity) was based on false information, which grew because there was nothing relevant to replace it, until today. People know that I am right, but the question remains: will they part with some of their great wealth or continue to live a lie? It will take only a few wealthy individuals to make the center a reality.

I am requesting $110 million from each wealthy person who decides to participate in this endeavor. However, if I fail to deliver on my promise, the bulk of that money will be returned to them since I am initially using only interest earned on it. As the center's wealth grows and my life promise becomes apparent, the $110 million will become the property of the center. What other organization gives you back money for failure to deliver? They shake your hand, give you a clap on the back, and smile all the way to their bank. What pathetic fools they must think the wealthy have become. I can just imagine the vacations they must have taken with the money donated by the wealthy.

As for myself, I am not taking a salary. This should be enough to shut up certain individuals.

What will it look like?

Much of the center will be below ground, which will enable staff, equipment, supplies, and so forth to move freely.

I would have included a building layout, but the architects most likely will change the buildings' location. For now, I will talk briefly about the buildings as I see them. Picture the main building with the other buildings on both sides running up to it. There will be approximately forty buildings of different sizes when the center is complete.

The main building, where the hub of activity occurs for the center, will be divided into three main floors and a basement. The basement will have dressing rooms and so forth for the cleaning staff, laundry, a receiving area for incoming supplies, bathrooms, storage, a tour guides' room, and underground parking for certain staff and guests.

The main floor holds the library, reception area, public relations office, employment office, bathrooms, orientation room, conference room, and global expansion room.

The second floor is mainly for staff offices and a large meeting room. Some of the positions included in the main staff are

- president,
- vice president,
- accountant,
- accounting assistants,
- secretary,
- receptionist,
- legal head,
- legal assistant,
- fundraising officer,
- grounds manager,
- global expansion officer,
- maintenance manager,
- public relations officer,
- retail manager,
- head of security,
- head of housekeeping/cleaning,
- architects,
- information and DNA manager, and
- employment advisory officer.

On the third floor are the presidential suites (high-security area), fitness room, and track. The suites are reserved for certain staff and special guests.

On the right side and facing the main building is the bulk of the sciences. Each of the sciences will have a research building and related buildings adjacent to them. In the beginning, suspended animation will have the largest number of buildings, as it focuses on above- and belowground patients.

Suspended animation will have a research building, suspension buildings, housing buildings one and two, a capsule research building, a capsule manufacturing building, an information and DNA storage building, and a small medical facility. It will also consider pet suspension. I saw a woman cry over the loss of a pet but hardly shed a tear over the loss of a close aunt.

The rest of the sciences' facilities to the right of the main building will include

- a resuscitation research building with a revival building and education building; an artificial organology building and a manufacturing building;
- a gerontology research building and a pharmaceutical manufacturing building;
- a cognitive reproduction and restoration building and an education building;
- an identity reconstruction research building with a DNA storage building, a DNA alteration and housing buildings, and a cloning process building;
- a regeneration research building; and
- a developmental biology research building.

On the left side and facing the main building will be other structures critical to the center's operation, such as,

- a bank,
- a property management building,
- an insurance building,

- residences (four),
- a security building,
- grounds and maintenance buildings,
- food fair buildings (four),
- a merchandise store, and
- a transplantation research building.

Seasonal staff will be needed when the center is open to the public, including

- orientation room greeters,
- merchandise store salespeople,
- fast-food restaurant workers,
- grounds and maintenance workers,
- cashiers for pay booths,
- parking lot attendants, and
- tour guides.

A block and brick manufacturing plant will also be located off-site.

I grow tired of trying to organize everything and look forward to the input of other staff.

What does the future hold?

There will be great action in the graveyards in the near future. A number of methods will be used to revive people from a death state, depending on their length of time underground. A person can be rebuilt from his or her deterioration point or cloned. Most likely, cloning methods will develop new ways to prevent health problems that have plagued individuals. At one time, I thought cloning would be almost impossible from a mental

The Afterlife

point until I realized that the average person is not a rocket scientist.

A combination of methods may be utilized, and the sciences will come up with those methods. An Egyptian mummy could be brought back to life, but the education process would be longer. The philosophy behind my thinking is simple: if you can preserve the human body, you can rebuild it.

The future holds many surprises, and we must be brave and bold enough to go after them.

CONCLUSION

There is more than one mistake in Christianity, but the major error is the death and resurrection of Jesus. The loss of two messiahs forced early Christians to be perpetual liars or else watch their religion deteriorate into nothing. Christ's body was the property of Rome, and Romans saw the power of messiahs to unite people. I don't think anybody knows when Christ actually died on the cross, but it was Romans who took his body down and placed it on a cart with the other dead bodies and then disposed of it. We know what the Romans did to the first messiah, Simon, and Christ came on the scene only approximately forty years later. The Roman mentality wouldn't have changed in that time.

Religious immortality was the only game in town, and it was easy for people to accept. A lie is as good as the truth if you have people willing to accept it. For something to have control over you, you must believe it. One must believe that when it comes to life, any chance to procure it is better than no chance at all. Today, there is a new chance to procure life, and it won't be long until many people choose it.

Everybody is conditioned to death, and I wish to recondition them to life, and only the Center for the Life Extension Sciences can accomplish that. If you want new alternatives that avoid death, then you must believe in the new variables of life that the center offers. Many people's vision and imagination are limited to the last book they read. They must learn to step outside the box if change is to occur.

I have always believed that one day the center concept and a person of great wealth would find each other and that the world would be a better place for it. My journey to this point has not been an easy one, but sometimes that's what it takes to achieve something of great importance.

Many people will give generously to the center once they see it as a reality or a soon-to-be one. Life is about to become the biggest industry on the planet, and the center will be its major instigator. What we are seeing so far is just the tip of the iceberg. The challenge to you and the center is to awaken humankind to the vast potential in human life that lies ahead. Institutions must learn to fire personnel quickly. Life is too important to have people sitting on their asses and accomplishing nothing.

People die because they want to, not because they have to. The center is a complete package and a one-stop shop for anyone seeking information on the sciences. The center's scope of research will be second to none, and its results will touch the lives of millions. No other research facility on the planet will have broken more ground in medical research and achieved more things than the center.

I have committed the better part of my life to discovering

new ways to save and extend life. Until my dying day, I will continue to honor life and work diligently to save it. To date, humankind has not spent the proper effort to get the results that the sciences are capable of delivering. People must be made aware of life's new options, and the center will be the instrument that brings that information to the world. I know the good that this center can accomplish; otherwise, I would have given up my quest many years ago. This center will either be our finest hour or the greatest regret that we'll take with us to the grave.

Being an immortalist, I adopt portions from all religions and beliefs in the hope that their teachings on morality will make me into a better human being. Immortalism is also key to the success of the center.

I failed to raise the $110 million from individuals to construct the center, concentrating on spending only the interest rather than the principle. Hopefully someone or someones reading my brief book can help. The quicker I obtain this amount, the sooner I can begin helping others.

All the things that I have mentioned and more will come about whether I receive the help or not. The trouble is that we'll both be underground waiting for a tomorrow that should be today.

Before writing this book, I spent a year in the hospital undergoing treatment for several ailments, including

- listeria,
- super bug,
- sepsis,
- COPD,
- vasculitis,
- pneumonia,

- avascular necrosis, and
- stroke.

Being in intensive care with so many things wrong worried me. I watched other people die from just one of these things. This was number *nine*. My nine lives are up, but I still continue to push on. There is no need to advise people to change their situation unless one has a viable alternative to replace it. Hopefully I have provided enough information to convince you. If I have, maybe I'll earn the title of father of immortality.

Please remember that the Center for the Life Extension Sciences will open its doors to a new branch of medical research focusing on a better understanding of death and how it can best serve our needs.

I wrote this book in the hope that it will successfully attract several wealthy individuals to the center's endeavor and convince them to be major players in its construction. Never in the history of humankind has such an important request been made. I promised you life, and the center will not disappoint you. The center will deliver much to your satisfaction, and your growth as a person will see new boundaries.

Printed in the United States
By Bookmasters